Table of Contents

———⊶∞∞⊷———

This book is dedicated to all who extend a helping hand to any one in need, without expecting any rewards in return.

Appreciation is extended to all who participated in sharing their story for the benefit of others in need of a simple intervention in a time of crisis.

Introduction

Life's Challenges

N early every family, in its journey through life comes face to face with challenges and crises which are so overwhelming that every bit of coping power is sucked out of the life of that family. So, it's shattered, hopeless and left with the feeling of being abandoned by family and friends.

The experiences in this book are real. The family I am writing about battled with their addicted father and husband as well as the depressed mother and wife. When they realized that they were not alone in the fight, but that others had the same problems, had recovered, and were ready to help them towards recovery, it was then that hope sprang up in their breasts. In that moment, they mustered the courage to get up and resist the pressures to implode.

Loneliness is a killer. One way to beat your depression and loneliness is to reach out and show another scared and lonely person that you, care. This book gives lessons in how persons in need found coping power to beat depression to the ground.

Friends Can Help You Cope and Overcome Life's Challenges!

A common golden thread of hope runs through this book as each participant comes to grips with very serious personal issues of health, addiction and loneliness. It shows what can happen when friends rally around those who face their crisis moment. A reason not to give up or give in replaces a tempting desire to roll over, surrender and die. These pages share the power of intercessory prayer. With positive results experienced, the desire to share the success story has resulted in the preparation of this book.

In this book you will discover victory and success in the lives of individuals who at times had a reason to give up on hope but found friends who walked with bags of hope, faith, and prayer and were willing to share it. Their experiences and life lessons can empower you as a neighbor to help others and receive their help for victorious living.

Part 1

Kamal and Fiona's Story

Chapter 1

A BROTHER'S KEEPER

Thou shalt love thy neighbour as thyself.

(Mark 12:31)

L ife is never straightforward. At times one can feel that he has made a fool of himself or that someone is trying to make a fool of him.

Sometime ago, I successfully made a fool of myself by jumping to conclusions in which I made a judgment about a gentleman without all of the facts. I really didn't know at the time if information was withheld deliberately or if the persons involved thought that the partial information shared was adequate since I was a newcomer to the church. I was told that the gentleman was an alcoholic. He told me so himself, when we first met and shook hands.

The next time I saw him, he was standing in front of a group of teenagers as their teacher. It was then that I jumped to a conclusion as I sat at a distance and watched the action. What came to my mind was, "What in the world could that alcoholic be teaching those youth seated in front of the church and in front of me a non-drinker. Who could have been so crazy as to appoint an alcoholic as a teacher of the youth class and then leave him and them alone without a chaperone to listen in on what he was teaching?" I do not know if from the distance he saw my focus in his direction and the oversized question mark etched on my brow.

However, after church that morning, as I reached the exit, there he was again with his hand outstretched and a big toothless smile. When he spoke, the words formulated were an invitation to dine with him and his family. I was relatively new to the country and the church. No one else had extended an invitation. It was the same alcoholic teacher. Who was I to say "no" to such an invitation? So, I followed him home and met his wife and three daughters who had preceded him home.

They were quite reserved but friendly. The house and furniture were simple and so was the meal which was quite tasty. What happened after the meal, turned out to be of greater significance than the meal itself? It was the unfolding of a journey where battles were fought with alcohol and with family members.

Let me introduce you to this warring family. Kamal is the head of the family and with his wife Fiona, they are raising three girls. Kamal shared with me that he is an alcoholic. When he told me that, he confirmed that I was right in my early judgment of him. I sat up and listened more carefully as he proved my point. Then he added as a footnote a clarification. He said, "I am a recovering alcoholic, once an alcoholic, always an alcoholic."

Kamal continued, "I have the disease of alcoholism and therefore am perceived as an alcoholic in the present tense." When he continued, what he said was enough to pull the rug from under my secure little feet. He shared, "I have not touched alcohol in twenty-six years." Indeed, as he shared this good news with me, I realized that I had made a fool of myself to have judged the man who was a winner and who had a success story to share with the youth of the church and now with me. This perception and attitude was the philosophy which governed his life. It was a necessary posture which kept him from assuming that because he had gotten a victory over the habit of drinking, he was automatically cured.

From this point on, I will refer to Kamal as "KB." KB continued to explain to me his very colorful life as a practicing alcoholic. Not only did he have to get therapy, but also his wife and children had to attend therapy since they were victims of his anger and abuse when he was in a drunken state. I asked him if they also drank. He replied in the negative. My follow up question was, "Why should they be required to attend extensive therapy if they were not alcoholics?"

He responded that his family needed to understand him when he acted as a normal human person and also to be able to tolerate his misbehaviour without abandoning him when most vulnerable. In therapy, they learned how to be patient and empathetic and to be there for him in the down times. They understood the importance of forgiveness and their need to forgive him for the bad treatment and neglect which had become a regular part of their lives.

KB and his wife Fiona had invited me to their home and family and had shared with me their lunch. They also opened up one of the doors of their lives and behind that closed door were some dark chambers to be explored at some later time. We both had prior appointments and had to cut short the exploration as well as the revelation.

Chapter 2

An Invitation to Dinner

——∽∾∽——

S ome weeks later, after recovering from the whole experience of sharing, my wife and I decided that we should reciprocate and invite KB and family to have lunch with us. I must confess that although I was curious to hear more of the journey, I was skeptical to do this because during our first meeting and discussion, he mentioned that when he was under the influence, he could be quite violent and out of order. At that time, I took seriously his statement that he was still an alcoholic. Suppose he took a shot of alcohol before coming to our home. Suppose he had a violent episode while waiting for lunch to be served? I did not feel physically or psychologically ready for such an encounter. I spoke to God about the matter and decided that he had been my protector throughout my life and should be able to do so again.

A certain peace overshadowed the afternoon and all started off rather well. Shortly after grace was said, KB posed a question about the drink. I had made the concoction from various juices and in my estimation the drink was entitled to a good grade. I observed that he had not yet tasted his and therefore I could not fathom the relevance of the question. Visitors usually request repeats of my drink. Why was he asking questions? Was he expecting something stronger? The question about the drink was, "Does it have any Angostura bitters in it?"

I must confess that sometimes I do put a few drops of Angostura bitters for flavor. Fortunately, I did not use any with the drink. By then, the two wives waited expectantly as the two men talked as men do. KB finally explained the reason behind his question about the drink. Angostura bitters has a percentage of alcohol in its composition. KB assured us that he exercises the utmost care not to partake of any beverage which has any alcohol at all in its composition. Since Angostura bitters has a percentage of alcohol in it formulation, KB chose to stay away from it for fear that its use may resurrect a desire to return to alcohol. This was another piece of the puzzle shared with me. It helped me to understand and appreciate his twenty-six years of abstinence. I found it very interesting and began to ask the question, "How can this system be applied to other addictive problems?" It called for a sensitivity to any stimulus or trigger which could precipitate a return to an old habit.

After lunch, we assumed a more relaxed position away from the table. We continued to chat more freely. KB opened a new door and invited me to enter. In this room, I saw and heard some new revelations. KB told me that he had to be institutionalized for his alcoholism. At the Alcoholic Treatment Centre, he was introduced to a process which should help him on his journey in coming to grips with his disease. From the second day after admission, the following regime was to be followed. He had to acknowledge that he was an alcoholic because he drank alcohol. From my vantage point, this did not seem to be a very earth-shattering bit of news, but for him, it was a very important first step. With some hesitation, he proceeded to share with us his deep thoughts about his problems.

Chapter 3

The Disease of Alcoholism

———— ❧ ————

K B confined, "I have the disease of alcoholism. Whenever I drink or eat anything with an alcoholic content, I have the desire for more. I have an allergic reaction that triggers an obsession and a compulsion to have more and more to satisfy the cravings.

"At some point, I surrendered and decided to do whatever the staff suggested was necessary for recovery. I was told to say the following: 'God, help me to stay away from the first drink today. No drink and No drunk today.'

"In the evening, before going to bed, I must say, 'God, thank you from keeping me away from the first drink today.' I did not have to believe in God to say that. Since it was not required that I believe in God, I said it every day and it worked.

"When I was discharged from the ATC, I was told to say: 'God, help me to stay away from the people and the places I was accustomed to. God, help me to go to Alcoholic Anonymous meeting today.'

"Without any pressure being applied to me, I found that I was gradually coming to believe that there was a God or some higher power that was beginning to impact my life and keeping me sober. I began to reflect on some episodes in my drinking binges when I was saved from death on several occasions. Worse yet, I was kept from killing other people including my own wife and two daughters. There must be an overseeing Providence.

"One Friday evening as I came home from an ATC meeting, I decided to have worship with my wife and children. This was the evening following a quarrel I had with my wife that morning. During the day I made the decision that at worship I would ask both God and my wife to forgive me for the things I said during the argument."

Chapter 4

The Desire to Kill My Wife

K B continued his story about his journey as an alcoholic. I was somewhat spellbound by his narrative. He shared,

"As I sat in my chair and awaited the commencement of worship, my head began to feel like an inflated balloon. It was then that I heard a voice shouting to me, 'Kill your wife.' My wife was sitting on my left. I could not understand what was happening to me. Quickly and quietly I said, 'God, please help me.' I chose not to tell my wife about those thoughts which came to me. I was afraid that she might decide to have me committed to the psychiatric hospital and I was not ready for that.

"Some time elapsed as I struggled to live a proper life and to treat my family as a good family man and husband should. It was not always as easily done as I thought it should be. One Friday night, as my wife and I lay in bed talking, she brought to my attention that earlier in the day I acted annoyed about something. I denied it while she insisted that I was angry that morning. Well that started an argument that neither one was prepared to lose. I decided to get up from bed and attend an AA meeting. After the meeting, I spoke with God and pledged that on reaching home I would apologize to Fiona for being so stubborn. Unfortunately, on reaching home she was already asleep so I decided that I would do it in the morning.

"When morning came, the idea of an apology was no longer on the agenda. I decided that an announcement to the whole family that we will be going to church together today. To this suggestion, Fiona said, 'No. I am going alone as usual.' Usually, she went ahead because she had some chores to attend to and when I decided to go to church, I took the children after attending to some domestic responsibilities. There was something about her reply to me that triggered an angry response in me. When she came from the shower, with the towel draping her body, the thought came to me to take the towel and place it around her neck while asking her a few questions. 'Are you serious about your answer to me that you are going to church alone. You want to send me crazy or something?' A message came through to me loud and clear at that point, 'Kill her.' I became so afraid and I released her.

"Before leaving for church, I called the children together and told them how very sorry I was for my behavior and angry display in their presence that morning. For the first in many years, the tears flowed from my eyes and with a broken heart; I cried out to God to help me stay sober and to live a better life. It happened on that day when I had decided to go to church with my family and engage in the worship of God, that I was beginning to understand myself and what God was doing in my life."

After such an exhilarating post-lunch session, I was not sure whether I should be afraid of the man with such potential to extreme violence or sympathize with him and his family.

Fiona, his wife, along with my wife Althea joined us during this sharing session. Fiona seemed quite conservative, passive and accepting of her circumstances. It is so easy for one to take a book by the cover before reading the contents. She had a captivating golden smile. When she started to express herself, she poured out her feelings of hurt and fear during the years when KB was drinking. She expressed her concern that the children would be permanently hurt by the years of abuse they witnessed and the neglect they experienced. She spoke of having to go to therapy and that the children were a part of the rehabilitation efforts. That day she felt more assured because she saw the progress KB had made, and she was thankful to God that such was possible. What was encouraging also was that in spite of the challenges, the family was still together and supporting each other

For me, that day was more than an eye opener. It was an education for me in understanding the struggles and the pressures families face when a member gets trapped in the cobwebs of alcoholism. This was the closest I had come to a recovering alcoholic. I have known of alcoholics who were not ready to admit that that they had a problem and were prepared to maintain the status quo of regular consumption of alcohol on the assurance that they could stop at any time they chose to do so.

My First AA Meeting

KB promised to invite me to an AA meeting. I gave serious thought to accepting the invitation. I was not sure what to expect or how one should dress for this first visit. I even wondered what my friends would think, perhaps that I had an alcoholic problem which was kept secret. KB was a confident man. He assured me that there was absolutely no reason to be apprehensive. He assured me that attending the meeting would be alcoholics in recovery. They were from all levels of society, from those with class as well as the classless.

The night of my first visit was a Thursday. I dressed casually and arrived early to make an assessment of the situation and to choose where I would sit for comfort. I soon became aware that the meeting was not Tobacco Anonymous. As the room filled with men it also filled with tobacco smoke. KB eventually came over to me and welcomed me to AA. He encouraged me to relax and observe. I exercised every effort to do just what he said.

At the appointed time, it was KB who called the meeting to order and chaired the meeting for the evening. When the basket was passed for the voluntary contributions and dues, he advised me not to contribute. That evening I sat and listened attentively to men who willingly shared their challenges, frustrations and failures. They also shared their victories and encouraged each other in the pursuit of victory. They were not ashamed to share their failures for they were all standing on the same ground. That night I attended AA, KB was in charge of the meeting. He had not tasted alcohol for the past nearly thirty years. His was a success story and now he had dedicated his life to help others experience the thrill of victory.

Chapter 5

Fiona's Struggle

F iona had her own struggles while her husband KB was being rehabilitated. Her greatest revelation during this time was realizing that she had real personal needs and unresolved issues. She forgot herself and completely absorbed herself in helping her husband and children come to grips with the challenges of being normal in a very abnormal situation.

This is how she expressed herself. "After my husband came in contact with Alcoholics Anonymous, I determined to do everything to make sure that he did not relapse and return to drinking as before. For me, it was difficult. Here he was, trying hard to succeed, putting forth every effort and really seeing progress to the point of being self righteous, I thought He was doing all the right things and doing the required things right. For me, I had stopped going to church and given up contact with my best friend. But over a period of time I only felt more and emptier as well as losing the ability to cope with the daily challenges of running a home and caring for my family.

"After some time in some state of numbness, I mustered the courage and told KB that I was thinking of returning to church and renew a spiritual relationship with God. My husband's response to this shared information was, 'Are you sure you don't want to wait for me?'

"My reply was a straightforward, 'No.' I was not sure how long his recovery would last and I was not prepared for any embarrassment. I took the children with me and left for church hopeful that I would begin to experience a feeling of peace and contentment. Unfortunately, the more I tried and the more I searched the less satisfied I felt. Happiness kept being a step or two ahead of me and I just couldn't catch up with it. I became angry. I felt that I was making the necessary personal sacrifices to help my husband and young children survive alcoholism and its affects and here I was all wrapped up in a cocoon of depression, anger and frustration.

"I loved my husband and children and anything that I needed to do for them and their well being, I was ready to try but nothing seemed to be working for me. What next could I try? Friends from Al Anon and church tried to encourage me with such words as, 'Let go and let God,' or 'Live one day at a time' or 'Easy does it,' and 'But for the grace of God,' filled my ears by those who did not have my problem and who were wives of alcoholics in recovery. The more they spoke and encouraged me the more anger, hatred, and resentment grew within me.

"It was my birthday. I arose early from sleep and started my day's activities of baking, cooking and house cleaning. KB, who was improving so well with AA's help, planned to have some of his friends over for dinner. He was entertaining his friends and for some reason, I was so angry and sorry for myself I decided that under those conditions and with the feeling I now had, I should stay away from company.

"I decided to go to bed. When I awoke from sleep, my husband had left for work. Dishes were in the sink, so I washed them and cleaned the house. The following day, all hell broke loose. I took the rolling pin and smash everything in sight. The children were there and witnessed their crazy mother in action. They began to cry with fear. I didn't even have the desire to hug them. I must confess that after expressing and relieving my anger, I felt must better.

"This episode in my life baffled me because I was not the alcoholic. By this time, my husband was getting his life under control, but now I was the one reacting to these horrible feelings. How could I be delivered from a repetition of such feelings and the uncivilized way in which I tried to express how I felt? I became a nag. I nagged and nagged my husband. The more I nagged him, the more he ignored my behaviour and the nicer he acted to me.

"I could not understand what was happening to me. Was I losing my mind? Why should I be going crazy when I am not the alcoholic? Why should my husband who was an alcoholic behave better than

I was? I nagged the children. I longed for the father and my husband to care for us as he should. He was trying and succeeding while I was collapsing. One day out of the blue, I came out of the bath and dressed for church, he came up to me and grabbed my towel and announced, 'We are all going to church today.'

"I said, 'No we aren't.' He replied, 'You really want me to get angry?' I knew what he could do when he got angry. Although he never stuck me or abused me physically when he was angry, the verbal abused was worse than a physical one. It was not going to be good if we were both angry at the same time. I am so glad that a serious encounter was averted that day. This became more important to me as time passed and KB, in a moment of relaxation, shared with me that on the morning of the towel episode, he heard a voice saying to him, 'Kill her.'

"Fortunately, he was sober and realized that what he was hearing in his ears was not of his own mind or desire. He shared with me that when he realized what was transpiring he became scared and decided to release me. In his remorse and shame, he proceeded to empty his heart of all the pain that had accumulated over time. He apologized and expressed how sorry he was for his behaviour. I accepted it and forgave him.

"Unfortunately, that day's encounter had its side effects. I developed the feelings that I was the responsible one and so feelings of guilt began to overwhelm me. I began to blame myself for being thoughtless and selfish. I was doing things to trigger those reactions in my husband. I opened a door of self blame, entered into it, closed it behind me and bolted it. I did not drink. I was not an alcoholic but the way I felt and acted made me believe that I had caught the disease.

"Self-pity kicked in and I had no answer for me. At home I was collapsing. Would my church friends be able to see through my pretence? I am a proud woman and trying to present these two faces was becoming too strenuous to be sustained over a long period.

"With my door closed to myself, I lived in a self-imposed prison. I had a feeling of security from any intrusion. My own thoughts had me prisoner. KB was attending AA regularly. Over a two-year period, I noticed he was changing. He had gotten victory over the bottle. But more than that, he was showing caring qualities of a loving husband and father. That should have made me happy but instead I was feeling worse.

"How could one who was an alcoholic and so out of control when he was drunk could be so loving, kind and thoughtful and one who had decided to be a church goer along with our children was losing control of herself? He was succeeding and I was becoming a bigger failure and unable to live up to what I really wanted to be. I really wanted to be a good wife, a better mother, and of course, a better Christian person.

"As a child, I had experienced the affect of alcoholism in families. I grew up near a rum shop where those who drank got together to drink and have fun. As I observed them, it seemed as if they were having fun. I concluded that these people were happy and I wanted to be like them. They talked, laughed, played dominoes, and drank themselves drunk before struggling home to their families. But they seemed so happy while they sat together as a support group. It was when they stood up and tried to walk, that the effects of alcohol on them became more pronounced. When they were together as a group and talking their nonsense, they laughed and joked at each other and no one felt threatened or hurt by the teasing. They acted like over grown school boys. I admired them and wished to be like them, to find a man to become my happy and fund-giving partner in life.

"Something changed between the time the group left the rum shop and the time they arrived at their separate homes. When they stood up to walk, their power to walk and to control themselves had all evaporated and left them vulnerable and helpless bundle of living clay trying to reach home with pockets empty of the money for groceries and bills. The brain was not functioning as it used to. Trees seemed to be walking towards them and vehicles were travelling where pedestrians used to walk.

After many close calls with vehicles, home was eventually reached.

"Home at last. There is some comfort with being at home but there is a mixture of trepidation with the feeling of security. At home, one can do some of the things one tries not to do in public. One can collapse on the floor and sleep fully dressed. One may even ignore the taunting of a wife and fear of children. At home one can mess up and feel comfortable until tomorrow. But more than that, one may be subjected to constant reminders of failures. There is a feeling that wife and children will be more bark than bite for in the morning all will be well again.

"The hangover will be gone again. The house mopped and cleaned and clothes are changed. There is a lingering desire to be back in the company of the boys at the bar, but it is nice to be home.

"KB was the man I got and where we were today was a side effect. My husband became seriously involved in the AA. He decided to take the two children in with him to the AA. For me, I was going to church and that was enough. After about two years attending the AA meetings, he mustered the courage to tell me that AA also had a program for the family called Al Anon. I decided not to attend with them. I was going to my church and that was that.

"I knew that I was not happy. I felt that much was missing in my spiritual life but to accept that I needed a different perspective on our escalating family issues was as far from my mind as the east was from the west. But KB was not giving up."

AA to the Rescue

"One day KB and one of his friends tricked me into going to a convention sponsored by AA. I decided to attend and be supportive of his efforts to improve his situation. Once at the convention I was introduced to a lady who befriended me and shared with me information about Al Anon, a program for families for alcoholism recovery. I never heard of such a program before. The lady was nice and friendly. She made me feel at home and comfortable.

"From that day on, every last Saturday night in each month, I have attended the meeting of Al Anon. I arranged to leave the children with their grandmother so I could attend regularly. Al Anon like AA used the Ten Step Program. I attended the meeting but did not observe the Step Program. I went to the meetings to get information but not to change anything I believed or was already doing. At one time when I was beginning to feel I had enough, my husband got the opportunity to relieve an AA officer who had to go out of town. My husband was asked to chair the meeting. Guess what? He asked me to accompany him to the meeting to see how he would conduct the meeting and give some feedback. I sat in the office and listened to the conversations as alcoholics and drug addicts came in and talked with him. I listened as they expressed their pain and a desire to overcome their addiction. At times, he even visited the homes and the friends of those who were suffering as I was suffering.

"It was then that I made the decision to do something about me and my problems. I started to practice the instructions given in Al Anon. I had listened to people who were trying to help me and were using certain words, catch phrases and sentences with the hope that they would help me. Words such as 'Easy does it,' 'Live and let live,' 'Let go and let God," 'One day at a time will do the trick.' All those cliché along with 'God's grace is sufficient for you,' were like pouring water on a duck's back.

"From my first attendance to Al Anon, I got the perspective that my first responsibility was to me not my husband and his alcoholism. Prior to this insight, it was my feeling that my responsibility was to help make my husband better. I was advised that when I am better and well I could more easily help anyone including my husband. He was attending his program regularly, and I was attending Al Anon on a regular basis.

"Together we have grown stronger than ever before. Alcoholics Anonymous and Al Anon have helped us and our children to understand the negative impact alcohol and drugs can have on the users as well as the families of those who do not use them but never the less are subject to the fallout from these drugs.

"We have been clean for more than thirty years and our children are now adults with their own families. We have organized programs to help families who have suffered or are suffering like we did. Our commitment now is to help as many of our brothers and sisters as possible. This has given us so much satisfaction through the years as we see the transformation that is possible to us who share as well as in the lives of those who receive our love and care. *Indeed we are our brother's keeper*. That brother you reach out to help may be your very own flesh and blood in need of your love and attention.

"There are so many beautiful stories and quotes that have been preserved whose authors are not known. These stories have encouraged many people along their personal journey. The following story is one of them which I heard.

"*I was walking down a dimly lit street one evening when I heard the screams coming from behind a*

44

clump of trees. I paused and listened with curiosity. It did not take long for me to conclude that something was amiss and that the screams were coming from a woman and she was in some difficulty. My heart raced while my mind tried to untangle the confusion. Should I get involved and move to the rescue? Should I leave the scene as quickly as possible and escape for my own life? I was not very athletic or muscular. Suppose I got involved and lose. The moments passed so rapidly and the cries of the woman became softer and softer. How could I walk away and be free with my own conscience that was now questioning my desire to run away and be safe? The time to act was now or never. I decided to play the man regardless of the outcome.

I rushed to the scene and pulled the man away from the woman. A wrestling match ensued and we were soon entangled on the ground as the woman escaped and hid behind some bushes. The man got up and ran. When I got my composure, I saw the woman hiding behind the clump of bushes. I assured her that all was well and she was safe. She took some time to compose herself and cautiously came towards me. In the dark, I could not see her face. Then she spoke, 'Dad, is that you?'

"Coming towards me from the darkness was my own daughter. The one whose life I saved was my own child's.

"Am I my brother's keeper? You bet I am."

Part 2

—❦—

Rosie's Story

Chapter 6

I Don't Know Much about God, But, I Believe in You

T hese words were expressed by my neighbour after she received words from her doctor that she had only six months to live. When she shared that bit of bad news and expressed her hopeless and helpless situation, I expressed to her that the least I could do for her, as a pastor and her neighbour, was to arrange an anointing session for her. I tried to explain to her that such a sacred service required a level of faith in God by the recipient. She was practicing everything except being a Christian. She attended her séances. She had read her books about the occult; received mass as often as convenient for her. Now she was dying, and I had become her neighbour and friend. Her response to the suggestion was a hopeful, "I don't know much about God, but I believe in you. So, go ahead and arrange the faith healing anointing."

This friendship developed over a period of time and with some reluctance. When my wife and I visited the house to which we were assigned, I met her. It was a lovely and warm summer day and she was in her garden. I deliberately went out to her as she attended the many beautiful rose bushes in her garden. I introduced myself as a prospective tenant of the house next door to hers and the possible chance of being her neighbor in a few days. Her body language did not reveal any excitement in having nice neighbors. Neither did it betray much resentment to the prospect.

She shared with us that she anticipated our coming because at her last séance, she got the information about us. She proceeded to tell us that the house we were to occupy was where she used to live. There was no wall or fence separating the two properties, so I envisioned a future that would not be free from neighborly interaction whether we wanted it so or not.

Thoughts went through my head. Does she still have keys to the house? What kind of séance attending, Catholic and English neighbor was I getting? Or what kind of Afro-Caribbean, Seventh-day Adventist neighbor was she going to get? We decided to play it by ear and be nice neighbours.

In a few days we were busy unpacking and setting up house. It was impossible not to come into contact with her on a daily basis since we shared a yard and no fence separated us. It was also a warm summer and there was absolutely no excuse for not enjoying the out of doors as time would allow.

As the days passed, our suspicions of each other gradually receded. She confessed that she was not very anxious to get too acquainted with us since we were religious and her prior experiences with religious people were not worth recalling.

She was a nurse at a hospital in the city, and had come into contact with Afro-Caribbean people before. She later revealed that they had ways of expressing their annoyance with her as a supervising nurse. Some of their methods used to express their feelings she was not familiar with at first.

For example when she gave some order that they did not agree with or did not appreciate, they had a way of stupsing their mouths without uttering words that would offend. She knew that this tone and noise bordered on insubordination at times but she was unable to write them up on any specific charge. This frustrated her because she knew the intension. She decided that she would find a way of dealing with them. With a twinkle in her eyes and a little smile, she shared with me, "I went home and practiced stupsing also and the next time they tried that with me, I turned and gave them a dose of their own medicine." This response caught them off guard and surprised them so it became a matter to be laughed at. Of course, this new experience made a significant difference in their relationship.

The fenceless common yard space provided many opportunities for us to meet each other. The warm weather and the blooming roses in her garden became a talking point. She had many varieties which she knew by name. I knew roses only by color, so for me this exposure was a learning experience as she became a teacher and I her willing student. Something good was happening to us. We were getting acquainted. We tried to exchange pleasantries and small talk.

Our suspicions of each other began to disappear completely and talk flowed more freely as personal things entered the conversation from time to time. As time slipped by and the days remained warm, we were invited to explore more of her garden which did show signs of having been cared sometime in the past but was now being overrun with bushes. We were introduced to the different varieties of apples, those that were best for eating and those for culinary purposes. In that garden were hives of bees which she kept. Rosie promised to show us how to harvest the honey. Classes promised to be exciting as we gradually opened our hearts to receive one another as neighbours and friends.

Rosie confided that she had been hurt by people who took advantage of her. She was afraid to open up her heart again to anyone. People could not be trusted. "Keep them at arm's-length for your safety," she said.

There were scars on the chambers of her heart and fears resulting from past unkind experiences which she encountered in her exchanges with fellow human beings. Audrey, my wife, and I decided to invite her over to our house on a Friday night when we had a little more time to relax. Our invitation was accepted. I must confess that I was not totally comfortable. In my mind, the thoughts kept surfacing, "What does she do when she goes to séance on Thursday nights? What sinister thoughts could she be cultivating about us in her mind?"

I did not know anything much about the occult or séance meetings and such like. I did not think it was necessary for me to take any classes at this time. So there were these very mixed feelings.

I felt ashamed of myself for thinking those negative thoughts. Why should I be concerned, anxious or afraid? Where was my trust in my God? It did not take long for my mind to be settled. I had advised many persons before that no one can harm another when God is with you and you placed your trust in Him. With that settled, a peace of mind came over me and my wife and our relationship with our neighbour continued to thaw from cool to warm.

Apparently Rosie was experiencing the thaw also, and she began sharing more of her experience with us. Attending séances on Thursday nights was not as exciting as before. She preferred to meet with our family on Friday nights when we met as a family to sing, pray, share experiences and worship God.

One Friday night, Rosie shared with us that during the week she had an experience that scared the life out of her. She decided to take some of her books on the occult, which craft and such like and make a bonfire with them. She knew how to light and manage a backyard fire. She had done it many times before. However, this time was different. Rosie lit the fire and moved to a safe distance. As the fire began to blaze, a ball of fire, in the shape of a man, left the pile of books and came in her direction and singed her eyebrows, lashes and some of her hair. She changed color from white to cherry red as she turned and with trembling steps hobbled to the safety of her house. She concluded that this was a diabolic reaction to her decision to burn those books.

She added, "Whenever I try to take up the Holy Bible and read from it, it crumbles in my hand and disintegrates. You can understand how I would have a problem reading the Bible."

Another phenomenon which happened to her was that all of her clocks would stop at the same time and restart together with the correct time. Rosie was scared, unhappy and did not trust man or God. Now she was our neighbour and we were not sure how to trust her.

Over a period of time we began to feel a little more comfortable with her. We continued to extend the invitation to her to visit with us on Friday evenings. These invitations were not refused so we concluded that she was opening her mind and heart gradually. We need not betray that growing confidence. We were quite careful in how we balanced our desire to reach out to help without creating the feelings of in-

truding into the private domain of one who was se-
verely scarred throughout her life.

Occasionally she would open a window and allow
us a glimpse into her painful life. She felt abused and
used by the men that came into her life. A daughter
she had given birth to was taken from her and adopt-
ed, and now her heart yearned to know what had become of that little bit of innocence. "Where could
my baby be now? Many years have passed I know.
She should be an adult. Is she alive? Is she happy?
Could I have given her a better life?"

So many unanswered questions; so much locked
up in her brain. "How do I relieve myself of the
guilt?" she wondered.

Rosie continued, "Sometimes when I think about
my past, the mistakes and wrong decisions I have
made when I was younger, I just feel so unworthy, so
unclean. I go to mass and occasionally confession to
the priest but return home with the weight still press-
ing me down. Some friends mentioned that cigarette
smoking helped people to deal with their problems. I
tried them too. When they did not work as I hoped,

I decided to increase the amount of alcohol beyond the amount I usually drank. I always kept at hand a supply of the best brands for a rainy day or an emergency. As a health professional, doing these things only added to the weight of my guilt.

"I tried not to become an alcoholic. As a nurse, I knew the importance of maintaining good health and a sober mind. The bottles are emptied over a period of time, but my mind remains full of my thoughts.

"With all of this to contend with, two adults with their two teenagers have come to live next door and are my neighbours. At my hospital, I have come into contact with West Indians. I supervise them. They have their own kind of English, which I don't always understand. Somehow I have gotten the feeling that when they don't want me to understand them, they talk in a certain way and when they want me to understand, they speak their English slowly and I get it."

My Other Neighbors

Rosie continued, "My new neighbors are West Indian. I am not supervising them. They live next door and regardless of how I feel or what I think about these people, they are my neighbours and there is no fence between our houses.

"So far they seem to be normal. They say that they have two children, a girl and a boy. The girl is studying in the U.S.A and will be coming home on holiday. The boy is in his early teens and friendly. They have invited me to their home on Friday nights. I wonder if they have séance that would save me from having to travel on Thursday night to my meeting place. I don't see so well at night, so going next door would be a benefit to me. I will accept their invitation and check it out.

"Well, that first night went better than I expected. I did not know what to expect. It was simple but effective. They welcomed me to their home and then introduced themselves by giving a brief introduction about Barbados, their homeland. I told them that

I was from the North of England, but lived and worked in the South for some time. After this chit-chat, they said that they were having worship and were welcoming the Sabbath.

"The worship comprised of singing hymns, reading scripture, prayer, sharing of experiences of life and events occurring during the week."

As Rosie continued to share, we learned more intimate details of each other.

Rosie shared that some nights she would have nightmares and would fall between the bed and the wall of the house. It took hours to un-wedge herself from between the bed and the partition.

The first worship session she attended went well. There was evidence that whatever frozen attitudes were there, it was breaking up as we reached out to each other. Rosie lived alone. Any family she had lived hundreds of miles away and few, if any, of her workmates visited her.

What should be our next steps? Rosie knew that we were a church-going family. What was different was that we went to church on Saturday instead of on

Sunday. We decided to invite Rosie to accompany us to church, and she surprised us by accepting our invitation. She seemed more relaxed than we were as we drew near to the church. At the end of the service, we invited her to have lunch with us. The response was positive also. At the end of the day, we casually asked her, "How was your day?"

With tears in her eyes, she quietly said, "It was one of the best days, almost perfect."

After we had said good night and closed our door, Audrey and I looked at each other in suspense. Here was a woman, our neighbor, hungry for friendship and we were given that opportunity to be a friend, our brother's keeper.

Taking Rosie to a Camp Meeting

Over the weeks, this interaction continued as often as possible. One evening, we mentioned that we were going to a camp meeting and would be away from home for ten days. We asked, "Have you ever been to a camp meeting?"

She said "No."

"Would you like to come with us?" we asked.

She paused and then replied, "Why not?" The drive to the campground took just over two hours. We reached the camp ground and quickly settled in.

We had made reservations for a simple bedroom with a sitting room for ourselves before extending the invitation. It was too late to make alternative arrangements. We agreed to give Rosie the bedroom and Audrey and I used the sofa in the sitting room. We thought that for ten days we could endure any inconvenience. But unfortunately, there seemed to be a problem developing. We suspected that Rosie was secretly crying. My wife and I discussed it and agreed that she would be the one to enquire what could be the matter. We thought that we were doing our best to keep her happy and comfortable. What were we doing wrong?

My wife mustered up the courage after a couple of days and enquired of Rosie what could have gone wrong. This question was the stimulus that triggered a whole new flow of tears. Rosie shared with Audrey that this was the first time in her life, that she could recall anyone making such a personal sacrifice on her behalf. For all of her life, she felt abused, taken advantage of or taken for granted. Today was so different. Someone seemed to care about her. She felt valued as a person and this made her feel like the person she always wanted to be; hence the tears.

Chapter 7

Only Six Months to Live

I t then became easier for Rosie to share with us her latest discovery; her doctor had given her six months to live. Six months to live! That was devastating news. This information came as a shock to us for more than one reason. We were being asked to return to Barbados to take up a new assignment. This was double bad news for Rosie; six months to live and less than six months with newly found friends, who were also her neighbours. The situation now presented a challenge to me. How could we leave our dear friend to face death alone? What could we do to make life and the threat of facing an unknown future less painful? I read James 4 again and decided to discuss the possibility with Rosie that the Bible gives an invitation to anyone who is sick and has faith in God to call in the church officers and request an anointing with oil after prayer and confessing of sins.

I discussed the prospect with Rosie and she agreed to accept it. Then she added, "I do not know much about God but I believe in you and you believe in God, so go ahead and make the necessary arrangements." I must confess that I had never heard it after this fashion, but I accepted the simple expression of faith and the challenge.

I talked it over with a fellow minister and set the appointment for the anointing. On the day scheduled, Roland, a fellow minister and I visited with Rosie at her home. We spent some quality time preparing Rosie for this very sacred and spiritual encounter; we assured her of God's love for her as one of His daughters. We talked of confession of sins, God's willingness to forgive and His ability to help any person to stop disobeying Him. We told her that Jesus is always extending invitations to any who is labouring and overwhelmed by the weight of their past mistakes. We assured her that God's primary work is helping sinners get victory over their sins and if she could accept this, we were confident that God would work in her behalf.

Again, Rosie's reply was," I don't know much about God, but I believe in you. If you believe it, I accept it with my whole heart." With this confession of faith, we proceeded to do the anointing. Am I my brother's keeper? Should I learn to love my neighbour as myself? Is it worth it? My neighbour must have appreciated this personal interest in her health and well being.

After leaving England and returning to Barbados, our separation could not signal the end of this new relationship. Every week the phone rang. On the other end was a British voice enquiring, "How are you? I hope you are well."

"I am doing okay," Rosie would reply. Rosie, who had never before travelled, had developed an eye to travel. Barbados was her destination. For six weeks she vacationed on the little island and enjoyed a new chapter on her life. She forgot that she was to have died in six months. Every morning she walked to the sea shore and enjoyed being tossed back and forth by the waves. She enjoyed her holiday as if it were her last.

In Barbados, an international evangelist was conducting evangelistic meetings. Rosie attended nightly. She decided that she must be baptized by immersion before returning to England. She insisted that I be the one to baptize her.

I cannot forget the morning of this event as she waited her turn with many others who had made a commitment of their lives to Christ. Tears of joy flowed as our minds tried to generate thoughts of understanding the change that is possible by the touch of the Master's hand in the life of a helpless person.

More than twenty years have passed and Rosie has not died. She has a reason to stay alive. Her health is not as vibrant as she would like, and she still lives on her own. We each understand better what it means to, "Love your neighbour as yourself." We understand how it feels when a neighbour extends a helping hand to someone in need of a friend, and that person responds as the sunflower to the sunlight. *I am my brother's keeper.*

"I was hungry and you fed me, thirsty and you gave me drink, naked and you clothed me, in prison and you visited me. In as much as you have done it to the least of these my brethren, you have done it unto me. Enter into the joy of thy Lord" (Matt.25:42-43).

Part 3

Fred's Story

Chapter 8

The Day Everything Crumbled

———∞∞∞———

F red had worked hard, very hard, for his Master of Science degree. For twelve years he taught science to elementary school children who did very well at inter-school science fairs. Parents enjoyed the success of their children and, the school relished the increasing good reputation for performance in science.

In the midst of such high water emotions, Fred felt that he needed a greater challenge. His application to teach Math and Chemistry at a high school was accepted. So, he said goodbye to parents, students and fellow teachers as he joined the staff at his new school.

Fred had received his Teacher Training Certification and had passed the exams and evaluations necessary to teach Math and Chemistry. His students testified that he had their interest at heart, for he not only interacted with them about academics, he also helped them come to grips with their personal challenges at home and in the community. Some of his students needed additional encouragement to stay in school and complete their high school requirements. Some others had to be helped to process their obligation to report to the authorities on their where- about. He enjoyed teaching as well as his preparation of assignments.

Fred became aware that he was having headaches periodically. These were treated as sinus problems, allergies or influenza symptoms of some kind. For his fortieth birthday, he decided to celebrate it with his family and friends. Approximately forty persons came to his home; some from the community, some from his school and other out-of-town friends. They had a grand time of pure fellowship. That was how his January ended, celebrating his fortieth birthday and being supported by family and friends.

By April, some changes were beginning to take place. The headaches intensified and an elevated fever accompanied it. This was unlike anything experienced before and Roena, his wife, decided to rush him to the emergency room at Delaware Hospital.

Preliminary tests of CAT scans and MRI's indicated the presence of a mass in his head that should not be there. The ENT specialist indicated that what was being detected and reprinted was not a negative mass and that further consultation was necessary.

What was developing was not information about the flu or sinuses, but a mass in the brain and where it was located made it more difficult for it to be surgically removed without possible damage to the muscles and nerves in the face. This might result in facial paralysis and he loathed the thought of having to live with that.

The primary care ENT specialist with whom he had the first consultation assured him that he had never seen nor had to perform surgery for the removal of a large mass so close to the face or brain, but he was prepared to take up the challenge. This information was quite necessary for decision making and they, Fred and Roena decided to seek further opinions at other nearby hospitals in Delaware, Philadelphia and Washington.

A neurosurgeon at Johns Hopkins Hospital was consulted and he referred the case to a fellow neuro-surgeon at Johns Hopkins, and an appointment was made with the ENT specialist.

A series of scans and x-rays were ordered. A study of them indicated and confirmed that there was in-deed a mass somewhere between the brain and the skull. The doctor took time to study the charts and consult with other specialist as to an approach. He informed the family of the serious nature and how difficult the surgery and procedure could be as the probability of further complication existed. Quite unfamiliar with the information, Fred and his family decided to share the news with other family mem-bers. This family has faced crises before and depend-ed on prayer and divine intervention. But this devel-oping situation was becoming a nerve-wrecking ex-perience.

Fred had just celebrated forty years of life. He was enjoying his profession as a teacher of science to high school kids. He has his own two children; one of whom is emerging into teen life and can't wait to learn to drive. She has been doing well at school.

The younger child, a son, was just six years old and he had his challenges with plastic surgery in order to correct a skull defect. He seemed to be fully recovered and functioning as a normal lad. Roena was the principal of a Junior High School. Would all of Fred's dreams, hopes, aspirations and even fears come to a screeching halt?

The news was shared with his parents; Fred was their only son. Would they lose him in the prime his life and career? How would his young family take this? So many thoughts and questions were generated. Fred asked his sister, Rakel, a nurse, to make the first contact with his parents and explain the situation, the procedures and possible hazards and fall out if anything went wrong.

One quiet and peaceful morning, the telephone rang and Fred's dad answered it. It was Rakel on the other end. The truth be told, I am Fred's dad. I could sense that this call was not a regular one. We did not usually get a call at this time of day from our children. We immediately picked up that something was unusual when we were asked to sit rather than stand. The hesitation in her voice betrayed that something was not normal.

Eventually the words slowly dripped out. "Fred is in the hospital and is undergoing tests. They suspect that there is a mass somewhere in the brain or near the brain."

"Kindly repeat," was requested. This was an attempt to process what was thought to be heard. She repeated the same message and this time it was absorbed and was making its immediate impact.

His mother walked away from the telephone and into the bedroom and there the tears flowed. Fred and his mom have had a very close relationship throughout his life. Time was needed in order to process this new and frightening news. I tried hard to remain calm and to think about the next step. I thought," if only it were possible for the situation to be transferred to me and set Fred free to look after himself and family, and to continue his career in helping young students." I felt that he had his full three score years and ten. Although I still enjoyed life, I would have preferred that the unfortunate situation would be his instead of our son's. This was impossible to barter.

The next thought would be, "How could his parents, so many thousands of miles away in the Caribbean be there at Fred's side and in full support"?

We shared the information with relatives, friends, and the church members. Prayers and intercessions for divine guidance were systematically organized. These began to mushroom as other friends heard of the situation and the serious implications. All over the world, as friends heard, they organized prayer groups and interceded for the physician as well as the patient.

We checked with Fred's wife and family as to the best time we should come to be with them. Where or when would be the greatest need, before, during or after surgery? Fred wanted to complete his school term, administer his examinations, correct papers and submit grades before the surgery. If all went well he hoped to be able to use the summer holidays for recuperation. If it didn't go well, the school had time to find a replacement.

In the meantime, his headaches increased in frequency and intensity. Perhaps the added pressures of meeting deadlines for school, attending the hospital for tests, take care of mortgages and bills all played their part in contributing to the additional headache pain.

In the midst of the many things to be done, decisions to be made, telephone calls began to come in. How could one not answer the phone at such a time?

The reassurance of prayer and offers of volunteer help did so much to remind us that although we live in a busy self-centered world, there are persons willing to help others carry their load to be a brother's keeper.

Chapter 9

Lord Teach Us to Pray

———∞∞∞———

T he disciples of Christ made a request of Jesus. "Lord," they asked, "teach us to prayer." This was our time to make such a request. For what should we pray?

The apostle James suggested that if any be sick, let him call up the elders and pray. The prayer of the righteous avails much. I have experienced situations in which prayers were offered and the patient did not survive or the situation was not reversed.

I have watched the televangelist proclaim cures in public healing. There are some well-wishers and admirers who would suggest that one wait and let nature take its course.

Others have their own home-made natural concoctions which they are anxious to recommend; confident of their potency. And there are still others, who without solicitation, express that they have no trust in the human physician, but only in the Great Physician.

In this kind of milieu of advisors, it is necessary to talk with God and ask Him to teach us how to focus our prayer.

There is much evidence in Scripture of divine interventions and positive responses to special requests for healing. There are records in scripture that God has gifted and equipped human beings to cooperate with Him in bringing healing to persons. These persons acted as God's agents to comfort and to heal.

However healing comes, miraculous or natural, God is at work. He works by direct intervention or He gives the person in need opportunities to cooperate with his agents. Elisha prayed and performed CPR on the widow's dead son, and he lived. A prophet was advised to make a poultice and apply it to a sore; then healing occurred. Jesus used an ointment on the eyes of the blind man and sent him to wash and receive his sight. He followed the instructions and returned seeing and happy.

Namaan was instructed to dip seven times in the river Jordan before he was healed. Reluctantly, but with some encouragement from his support group, he received that which he wanted most. He was restored to full health. Elijah was God's agent and the method, though unorthodox, worked for the believing patient. Sometimes there was the miraculous and direct divine healings. Jesus visited Peter's mother-in-law who had been sick with a fever. He restored her life to full bloom.

Coming down from the experience on the mount of transfiguration, Jesus, with three of His disciples, walked into a situation where some of His disciples tried to heal a demon-possessed boy and they couldn't. Jesus took over and saved them further embarrassment by healing the boy.

I have listened to many testimonies of persons who are confident that the doctor saw a growth or mass at some area in their body. They believed in divine intervention. Their friends lifted their case up to God in prayer and fasting for a divine intervention before the day of the surgery. Their testimony is that on return to the physician, no trace of the tumour was seen or found.

Many naturalists are confident that their natural remedies have potency and can be trusted to reverse even incurable health problems. Those who practice scientific medicine do not usually give them much credit. At other times, when measures are put in place to follow a better diet, and reverse years of abuse the body repairs itself over a period of time.

With all these possibilities playing hide and seek in the brain, how does one advise his son about the content of prayer? Should it be for a direct miracle or for the Great Physician to work through diagnostic and surgical experts at a hospital? Deciding what to advise and what steps should be taken was by no means an easy decision. Of course, there is a safe way to pray. Pray for the miracle and then add, "Thy will be done," so that one is covered in the eventuality that there is no external evidence that the prayer was not effective. The need for special prayer was shared with loved ones and friends as well as church memberships in different places.

We felt that the situation, as explained to us by the physician, was quite serious. It was not a limb to be amputated or an appendix to be removed. It was a mass in the area of the brain and the specialist physicians requested time to study the x-rays thoroughly and for further consultation with colleagues.

Almost automatically, on hearing of the situation and the technical nature of the surgical procedure, support groups began to form. Prayer groups went to work in Barbados where grandparents lived. At churches where Fred and his family worshipped in the U.S., prayer groups were organized.

Friends solicited the help of the Three Angels Broadcasting Network to include Fred in their international prayer roster. Friends used their houses for prayer sessions.

In the meantime, we, the parents, arranged to travel from Barbados to Delaware to assist resident relatives and friends in taking care of domestic chores before the day of the surgery. The children had to be supervised during hospital visits. The lawn was to be mowed and children taken care of. Roena still had unfinished school business to attend to. Pre-surgical visits and testing required her presence. Roena's parents were a great source of strength and support throughout the family crisis.

Three different families and friends within fifteen to twenty minutes of the Johns Hopkins Hospital called and volunteered their homes for us to stay from the day of the surgery until the day of his discharge from the hospital.

Many of Fred's friends who had attended his fortieth birthday party called him to say that they would be there for him and would come to his home to spend the last week-end with the family before the surgery. There was such a spontaneous outpouring of support from friends and loved ones that there was little time to think about surgery and the prospect of failure.

Chapter 10

Fred, the Planner and Organizer

———∞∞∞———

W hen Fred was in primary school, he demonstrated that he was well organized in his mind. He kept his room tidy and had a place for everything, and kept everything in its place. His socks and under-things were kept folded and neatly arranged in their separate drawers. His bed was made up before leaving for school. He tried matching his socks and pants. He had a problem walking with his dad, if his dad wasn't coordinating colors or if he thought that a particular suit or pants had outlived its usefulness. The news of his impending surgery triggered in him the many things he needed to set in order before he went to the hospital.

He prepared his will. He gave instructions as to who was to assist his wife, Roena, with the children. He wanted to attend his son's graduation from kindergarten. His daughter's sixteenth birthday was coming up and he wanted to celebrate with her. He arranged to have his students take their exams and have their grades filed. His lawn must be impeccably manicured before he left for surgery.

All of this planning began to create in his family a sense of apprehension that he was planning and preparing just in case something went wrong when he was on the operating table. This brought additional sadness to his wife, who was reduced to tears whenever the thoughts came to her mind that there was a sense of finality in all of this.

Fred was too busy to engage in thoughts of sadness. He went about his daily duties and chores as if all was normal. His calm and cool demeanour kept all of his well-wishers from breaking down in tears. How could they express their sorrow or apprehension in front of him when he was so much in control with his situation? Was he in denial or just pretending that all was well while hurting from the storm raging on the inside?

To add to the drama of the situation, Fred, having been briefed by the doctors that the surgery was very technical, was very much aware that there was the probability that a number of things could go wrong in the surgery.

If the brain was accidentally touched during the operation, they would have to stop the procedure and do repair work on the brain before continuing to re- move the mass. It was also possible that certain mus- cles and nerves in the face and ears could be dam- aged, resulting in facial deformity.

The prospect of a facial deformity seemed to dis- turb Fred more than anything else. His reaction to this was to give instruction that if they were any fa- cial deformities or if he went into a coma, that after six days, the life support should be withdrawn. I sug- gested that he make it at least seven days, to which he agreed. He was also told that the procedure would take at least thirteen hours.

All of the above sentiments so clearly laid out, cre- ated in his family, relatives and friends a greater and more urgent need to pray for him. While everyone of his supporters, and everyone who really cared for Fred in the prime of life and at the height of his career was busy trying not to panic, he was as in control and cool as if he were planning to attend a ball game that might be cancelled.

The first date for which surgery was scheduled was April or May. This was not good, as Fred saw it, because it conflicted with the plans he had scheduled. Although he was suffering regular headaches with intensity and saw the need for immediate surgery, he wanted the month of June to do the things he had in mind before going to the hospital.

Audrey and I decided that we would leave Barbados and go to Delaware as soon as we were sure about the schedule for the surgery. Roena would have it really tough considering her work as principal of a school, occasional hospital visits for testing and taking care of the children during the pre-surgical time.

Doctors were consulting as to the best approach to the surgery. Suggestions of possible approaches were shared with the family. After a serious and deliberate evaluation of all of the charts, the surgeons reduced their options to one. They would approach the mass by way of the nostrils. Each approach had potential hazards.

During this time support prayer groups were busy interceding with God to do His best for the family, and especially for the patient. The first break through came when the primary doctor changed the proposed date and arranged a date which accommodated birthday celebrations for Elaine, who was turning sixteen, and the Kindergarten graduation for Siege Jnr.

It gave time for us, his parents, to come to Delaware and help with the many things to be done. Rakel, Fred's sister, flew in from Chicago to assist in planning the birthday party for Elaine and her friends. Fred met us, his mother and father, at the airport in Philadelphia. In the drive home, conversation was as usual. There was no semblance of nervous fear or any apprehension. We had to raise the issue when we arrived at his house and solicit information as to what was going on in his mind.

His cool and casual response was, "I have listened to the doctors. I am aware of the possibilities. I can't do anything to change the situation, so I am planning all I need to put in place and leave the rest in the hands of God and the physicians." As a parent, I just sat there and listened respectfully to my only son, forty years of age, 190 pounds of muscle. He was studying for his black belt in Karate and exercised to keep his body in great shape. I looked at him and wondered how this episode in his life would end. I thought about Abraham with his son Isaac on the altar about to be slain. It was then that a secret wish came to mind. Since I had lived already and passed three score and ten years, why could we not exchange places? Let him live. If one must go, let it be me.

I began to sympathize with God, who saw His son Adam facing death in the prime of his life. He and his wife Eve were enjoying life to the full when an intruder entered their home and changed forever the good thing they had going for them. They made a serious error in judgement and decision and now the result was the loss of almost everything that had meaning for them.

How could a Creator and loving Father let His son and daughter, Eve, just die? I heard Jesus volunteering, "Let me take his place; let me die so he may live." I got an eye opener of the efforts of the Godhead to do all possible to save an only son who faced death. The statement, "God so loved that He gave His only beloved Son," took on new meaning and new appreciation within me. God and company came to the rescue.

After Many Days

From childhood, I learned the following verse from Ecclesiastes 11:1: "Cast your bread on the water and it shall return to you after many days." When I did not know better, I would add to it the word "wet." I have lived long enough to realize that it can return very dry also.

Another very important bit of advice, warns, "Be careful how you treat others when you are climbing the ladder of success. You never know who you will meet on your way down."

Many years ago my wife and I had the privilege of living and working on the beautiful island of Antigua. Among the many people that befriended us was a teenager by the name of Paula. My wife took her under her wings. They became bonded friends, singing together and doing things for others in the church. When Paula completed high school in Antigua, she transferred to Barbados to study for a degree in history. By that time, we were already stationed in Barbados. Four years of study in Barbados provided the opportunity for Paula to become a member of our family although she lived on the campus of the university. As happens in life, we all parted company and went our separate ways as our careers dictated. Paula and Ronald, her husband, now live in Maryland with their adult children who are college graduates.

Clem and Veda, his wife have been our friends for many years. We met Veda in London when we lived there. Clem was a friend from college days. There are some friends that are very special and even though we do not correspond or communicate on a regular basis, whenever we meet we pick up from where we left off the last time we were together. Clem and Veda were those kinds of special friends. They now reside in Maryland.

These two families were special to us at this time when our son and family had a medical crisis. When it was decided that the surgical procedure would be conducted at the Johns Hopkins Hospital, both of these families automatically volunteered to assist in any way possible to make our stay as pleasant as possible. Each family lives within twenty minutes of the hospital. Each family invited us to stay with them overnight and avoid the hassle of travelling from Delaware on the morning of the surgery. This would have been stressful since Fred had to be at the hospital by five in the morning. It would have been financially difficult for all of us who wanted to be there to pay the hotel costs just to be near the hospital. Because of the two offers, our biggest problem was in making the decision which of the two offers to accept. We were confident that whatever decision was made would be acceptable to all. There is no tinge of jealousy between the families. We decided to stay with Paula and Ronald.

In this situation, we could not help but recall the story told by Jesus, that our heavenly Father is as interested in the wellbeing of the little sparrows so that no one should feel neglected. We felt like the sparrows for which God had made provision long before we thought that we would need such. In a short time, the Ramsey's, another family and friend offered transportation and other help as needed. Was all of this an accident or was it that God had been secretly planning for us in love and had placed his agents in strategic positions near Johns Hopkins in anticipation of our arrival? Does Jesus care that much? O yes He cares. He impresses upon human agents to join him in being a caring person. He commends caregivers for being involved in reaching out to those in need. He says that such extension of love to others is love extended to Him.

That Monday evening, the eve of the surgery, was more like a celebration than some sad or nervous occasion. Some seventeen people converged at the home of Ronald and Paula. Eleven of them would spend the night there. The others were there in supportive roles and would return to their homes after the evening's activities.

Paula enjoys cooking. As the custom was, when we rang the doorbell to announce our arrival, such a lovely aroma greeted us that we forgot how to be sad or anxious. We engaged in so much pleasantries and commendations. Shortly after, Fred and his family arrived. Fred looked like someone from another planet. The doctors had placed all of these markers all over his head and face where they would make the various connections to keep his head immobilized during the surgery. He looked like someone from outer space. His wife and children were with him and all looked quite relaxed and ready for dinner.

It did not take long for all to settle because we had visited that home and family before and were always treated like extended family. Jas and her Husband Jeff were there. They had volunteered to help us in any way necessary. They made their home available for housing and their car for transporting us to and from the hospital. Veda and Clem, her husband, was present. They too had volunteered to see us through this crisis. Clem, a pastor, was there and rendered pastoral and spiritual support that triggered a special peace and relaxed atmosphere.

When everyone was ready, we proceeded to give thanks to God for a number of things. The doctors had diagnosed the problem and had put together a medical and surgical team to deal with the problem. We had found a hospital within a reasonable distance from home in Delaware. The timing for the surgery was arranged giving the patient time to attend to family issues which he had on his agenda. Their families all within twenty minutes of the hospital were willing to accommodate us. This made life so much more manageable. We did not have to increase our debts by adding board and lodging to the costs.

After giving thanks to God, we turned over to our good friend Pastor Clem the rest of the time before attending to supper. He chose an appropriate portion of Scripture for assurance of divine care and then he petitioned God to continue to guide the physicians and their hands as they performed this very delicate surgery.

Early to bed and early to rise was a necessary choice after dinner. Fred had to check into the hospital by five a.m. in preparation for surgery at 7:00 a.m. All went well during the night so we were on time to check in at 5:00 a.m.

As human beings, we can't see around a corner, neither can we see the future. We are convinced that that the God whom we serve has planted support groups in strategic place for a situation such as ours. When it became necessary these families, our brothers and sisters came forward and volunteered their resources to make us all as comfortable as possible. For such services we are more than thankful. *We are our brother's keeper.*

There is a story of Frank Reed who was held hostage in a Lebanese prison during the years 1986 to 1990. For months at a time Reed was blindfolded, living in complete darkness or chained to a wall and kept in absolute silence. On one occasion, he was moved to another room, and although blindfolded, he could sense others were in the room. Yet it was three weeks before he dared peek out to discover he was chained next to Terry Anderson and Tom Sutherland. Although he was beaten, made ill, and tormented, Reed felt most the lack of anyone caring. He said to an interview with Time, "Nothing I did mattered to anyone. I began to realize how withering it is to exist with not a single expression of caring around [me]....I learned one overriding fact: caring is a powerful force. If no one cares, you are truly alone." Caring people provide the strength to endure.

Chapter 11

The Point of No Entry

A t four thirty in the morning, two vehicles made their way from the home of Paula and Ronald to the Johns Hopkins Hospital. It was a quiet and warm morning. There was little traffic on the route. Within twenty minutes, we were there. We found a parking spot but soon realized that the hospital occupied more acreage than we imagined. It seemed as though we were walking and running forever as we tried to locate the particular unit where Fred was to report. All along the way, we enquired about the direction and found staff quite polite an accommodating. We reached the correct unit eventually and checked with the one in charge. We had a large delegation, too large for the waiting room.

Fred was escorted to his room. This was a private moment for him and his wife who stayed with him. When the nurses completed their admission procedures and had all papers signed, then other family members were invited to come to the bedside. He was appropriately dressed in one of those gowns where the front is at the back. The markers which he had all over his head from the day before took on a more prominent appearance. Now we knew that he was an alien. He looked so much different from the rest of us in that room. We took turns and rotated the two persons allowed in the room and at the bedside.

We felt that these final moments prior surgery belonged to his wife and children. The rest of us waited patiently in the waiting room. The one in charge was so thoughtful and accommodating and sensitive to our emotions. She offered some snacks as well as some chat. We felt so at home. It was still early in the morning as we awaited the arrival of seven o'clock when he would be rolled into the surgical area, the point of no entry for us. We knew that time was running out. The minutes were ticking away. The realization that we would not see him again for some fourteen hours was quite a sobering thought. At around six thirty we were allowed to enter the room. At that time, the neurosurgeon entered and thoughtfully shared with us, the parents, the procedure to be followed and his confidence that all will be okay.

At this point in the conversation, Fred introduced us to the physician and told him that his father is a pastor and had prayed for the surgeon and the success of the operation. In humility, this specialist accepted the thought and expressed his appreciation for the prayers. I really thought that this was a sign of a great person and caregiver. It added so much to the confidence we needed as our son would soon leave our presence, enter the realm of unconsciousness while the doctors used their skills and hands to go through his nostrils and hoped to remove whatever was there without causing further damage to any other organ. It was the combined efforts of God and man working together to ease the discomfort of a human being.

Before the doctor departed the bedside, he took time to assure us all that reports will be shared with us every two hours. That was comforting news. We thought that this was so professional and thoughtful. The thirteen-hour wait would be broken into two-hour segments. This would be so much better for all waiting so anxiously in a waiting room, caring and helplessly waiting on someone we love so dearly.

At last the moment of truth had come. We were saying our goodbyes and wishing well. The attendants were wheeling our son away from us towards an unknown destination and we had reached a point where there was no further admittance for us or any other family member. He must go through this experience alone. When Fred was a child and attended the dentist, his mom was there to hold his hand. Today, that tender motherly touch would be absent. Subconsciously, his mind must reflect on past sharing of love and support in good times as well as not so good times. Those memories will bring him and us through. We were confident about that. So with repressed tears we said goodbye at the door marked, "No Entry."

Chapter 12

Waiting is Hard Work

———◈◈◈———

T hirteen hours is a long time to wait when you are not enjoying yourself. Thirteen hours is made up of forty six thousand eight hundred seconds and the same number of tick tucks of the clock. It is a long time to sit and listen to each tick and each tuck.

We had brought with us, courtesy of our friends, some sandwiches and some books to read, if we got in the mood for such. We retired to the waiting room assigned and began the wait. For a change, no one seemed anxious to start a conversation, so out came the paper backs. The silence was developing into a solid mass that could be sliced. This developing picture soon changed because in the distance a familiar figure was approaching. It was the charming niece who had brought with her the captivating little smile which she uses to diffuse any unwelcomed intrusion into her space. Akuna , a PH.D. research student at the Johns Hopkins Hospital, had taken time off that day to come and sit with us in that waiting room. She was not empty handed, for from her bag, she began to bring out some little treats which she proceeded to share with us. Akuna does not usually talk much so it was easy for her to fit into the sombre environment we were quietly creating. From time to time, she would proceed to warm up the chill by asking a question and allowing time for an appropriate response.

This too soon changed. The first two hours were expiring. One could hear the change in the breathing patterns. Deep breaths were inhaled. Anxious looks were focused towards the nurse's station. Don't they know that the two hours are nearly up? We had forgotten to synchronize our time. Of course, we had also forgotten that we were not the only responsibility of the hospital and staff. It is so easy to forget that so many other patients and concerned relatives were milling around just as anxious as we were.

Whatever direction our thoughts were leading us, was soon interrupted as a nurse approached and solicited our attention. She was bringing the update on the patient and the doctors. "Fred is doing well and the doctors are satisfied with the progress."

"Thank you very much. We appreciate it." The load of bricks that was on our chests trying to squeeze out every bit of air from our lungs became like a load of feathers. What a relief. That bit of early news was encouraging. The atmosphere in that waiting room changed automatically. Everyone had some comment to make. Appetites suddenly returned as one by one a decision was made to check out the sandwiches which were, until then, well sequestered in the security of a bag.

It was time for breakfast, and breakfast was served. The wait became easier to bear as the second time segment of two hours was anticipated. Fred's in-laws made waiting less stressful because they did the baby sitting with the children, and occupied their attention with things of lighter weight than school work. Roena was free to pace the floors of the hospital while the office clock took its time to mark off each two hour period. It must be a most uncomfortable feeling to think of one's husband lying helplessly on a surgical table with doctors probing through one's nostrils as the only route to remove a cause of much discomfort to a person cared so much about. She displayed no external signs of significant anxiety but stoically braved the tension.

Roena moved towards the nursing station as the second time period drew closer and closer. The messenger was not on time for the second announcement. Was anything going wrong? Did someone forget the promise? Other members of the support group stood up and began to paste the floor. Anxiety began to build. It was then that the second message came, some ten minutes after the expected time. Why should we think that two-hour time frame was a precise one? Why should we have thought that the nurses in surgery would stop in the midst of the procedure to send a message to waiting family and support group? Such questions and thought do make waiting hard work, and we were perspiring from the labor. Anyhow, be that as it may, the news was excellent news. The surgery was going well, the patient was cooperating and all was encouraging.

The day continued to unravel as each segment of time brought good news. After thirteen hours of waiting, we observed that the outside was darkening. We had come to the hospital in the dark, at dawn. It was dark again. Night had come. We began to think about the doctors. How tired were they by this time? We paused and breathed a prayer for tired doctors. They too have their children and families, but they are in surgery attending to someone else's child and husband and friend.

Thoughts of thankfulness began to emerge. There at work for more than twelve hours were human beings who had dedicated themselves to the saving of life and the healing of sick and broken bodies. This was the kind of work that Jesus did when he mingled with human beings in need of a physician. He went everywhere healing the sick and restoring of sight to the blind. Doctors and nurses are God's support staff and team in the same business of healing. We were thankful for them and their work to restore broken lives.

Finally, the wait was over. The chief surgeon appeared in person and delivered the final message.

"Surgery went well, better than expected. We were able to remove all of the mass and most of the shell that contained it. The patient cooperated well. You will get to see him as soon as he is cleaned up and out of the recovery room," he said. That good news was the best way to climax a day. How should we respond? Shed tears of joy? Scream and release the tension built up during the day? The hospital is a quiet zone, so that kind of noise is not appropriate in the hospital.

Self-containment was the order of the night. In a short time we were allowed to go to Fred's room, two at a time. Wife and daughter were the first in to congratulate the semiconscious recovering patient. He tried to talk but the sound did not follow the thoughts. We got our turn also before going home that night. Siegie, his son who was six years old, was not allowed in at that time. When he saw his grandmother, his question was, "Grand mum, did they cut off his ears. Does he still have a nose?" We quickly assured this questioning mind that all of these organs were still attached and that his dad was very okay.

That was Tuesday and Wednesday was approaching. When we returned to the Hospital on Wednesday, the doctors assured us that the postoperative evaluation looked good and that the patient would be released to go home on Thursday. This was more than a pleasant surprise and gift.

Within a few weeks, Fred was back to normal. A year after, well wishers still ask the question, "How is your son?" I visited the island of Dominica months later and was pleasantly surprised when a teenager stopped me and asked that same question. From every corner of the globe the question keeps coming more than a year later. "How is your son?" In all of my years, I have never experienced such an outpouring of support for anyone in need of pray and healing. We appreciate this network of support and the fact that God responded positively to their intercessions.

The thought that at no time does anyone have to feel alone in this big world is quite exhilarating. Anyone who cares and supports another human being gives that strength which is necessary to carry on until success is achieved.

Thanks for your support. You are your brother's keeper. I am my brother's keeper. We are our brothers' keeper.

The story is told of a German pastor by the name of Martin Rinkart who lost many of his parishioners during the Thirty Years War which was fought in Europe during the seventeenth century. In spite of the hardships and the suffering, he was able to write a table grace for his children. He pointed them to God who was worthy of their thanks. As a family, we too share similar sentiments.

"Now thank we all our God
With heart and hands and voices.
Who wondrous things hath done,
In whom His world rejoices.
Who from our mother's arms,
Hath led us on our way
With countless gifts of love
And still is ours today."

We thank our God for manifesting His caring and His patience in listening to the fervent petitions that ascended to Him daily on behalf of our family. We appreciate the caring and the support which came from so many, known and unknown. Our son is back to normal and has returned to teaching the boys and girls with whom he shares his story. They too have learned that in spite of the varied challenges of life, they are not alone. There is always someone there to help with the load.

We are our brother's keeper and it is good to let him know.

CPSIA information can be obtained at www.ICGtesting.com
Printed in the USA
BVOW021311170612

292836BV00001B/3/P